# The Country Kitchen

# BARBECUES

## Barbara Beckett

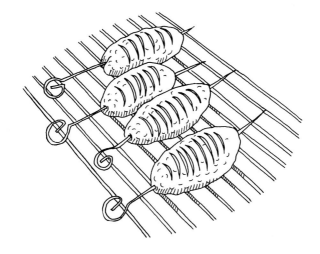

The Country Kitchen

# BARBECUES

*Barbara Beckett*

HARLAXTON
PUBLISHING

*Front and back of jacket: A barbecue lunch in the garden. From left to right, tabbouleh (p.44), Japanese chicken kebabs (p.34), country-style pork chops (p.22), barbecued vegetables (p.40) and roast sirloin (p.18).*

*Front and back endpapers: An old-fashioned country kitchen with the preparation for a spicy fruit cake in the foreground. The wood burning stove is wonderful for long, slow cooking.*

*Page 2: Country-style pork chops (p.22) sizzling on the barbecue, accompanied by baked tomatoes (p.34).*

 *COOK'S NOTES: Standard spoon measurements are used in all recipes.*
*All spoon measurements are level.*
*All ovens should be preheated to the specified temperature.*

*Fresh herbs are used unless otherwise stated. If they are unavailable, use half the quantity of dried herbs. Use freshly ground black pepper whenever pepper is used; add salt and pepper to taste. Use all-purpose flour unless otherwise stated.*

Published by Harlaxton Publishing Ltd
2 Avenue Road, Grantham, Lincolnshire, NG31 6TA, United Kingdom.
A Member of the Weldon International Group of Companies.

First published in 1992.
Reprinted in 1993.

Publishing Manager: Robin Burgess
Project Coordinator: Barbara Beckett
Designer: Barbara Beckett
Illustrator: Amanda McPaul
Photographer: Ray Jarratt
Editor in United Kingdom: Alison Leach
Typeset in United Kingdom: Seller's, Grantham
Produced in Singapore by Imago

British Library Cataloguing-in-Publication data.
A catalogue record for this book is available from the British Library.
Title: Country Kitchen Series: Barbecues
ISBN:1 85837 010 8

# CONTENTS

*Introduction*
7
*Starters & Drinks*
9
*Meats*
16
*Poultry*
30
*Fish & Shellfish*
35
*Vegetables & Salads*
40
*Desserts*
45
*Index*
48

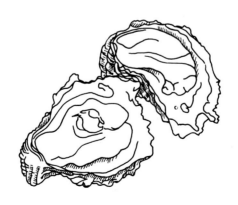

# INTRODUCTION

BARBECUE COOKING is the most ancient and primitive way of preparing food – and yet it is one of the most enjoyable. It satisfies a deep urge to get back to a less complicated way of life. Certainly, the participants are more aware of how the food looks, and their sense of taste is heightened as they stand around the fire breathing in the wafting, smoky aromas. It is fun to eat informally with fingers and to gnaw on the bones. It can be the easiest and most satisfying way to entertain friends and family of all ages at home or on a picnic and, if you marinate and prepare the day before, you can fully enjoy yourself at your own feast.

You will find recipes in this book for starters and drinks; beef, lamb and pork dishes; chicken and duck; fruit, vegetables and desserts; along with marinades and sauces to accompany them. There are helpful tips in the Cook's Notes that are worth reading for practical ideas. The recipes are written for 6 people but easily reduce or expand as you wish.

There is an art to good barbecuing that comes with practise. The first thing you require is a good fire with hot even coals and without flames. I haven't space in this book to go into detail on fire-lighting and the different types of fires and barbecues – but allow an hour to an hour and a half to get your fire hot enough to cook on. That is, the fire should have died down and a light gray ash should cover the glowing coals.

*Threaded chicken, chicken livers and peppers make up this delicious Japanese chicken kebab dish (p. 34). Serve with steamed rice and use the marinade as a sauce.*

You can judge the temperature of the fire by slowly and carefully lowering your hand, palm down, near the rack – if you can keep it there for 5 seconds, the temperature is low; 4 seconds, medium; 2 seconds, hot. Use indirect heat for large roasts.

Some cooking implements are essential. I couldn't be without long-handled tongs for lifting and placing small pieces of food; skewers for kebabs and satays; stainless steel spatulas for lifting large roasts – never pierce meat as it allows the juices to escape; a brush for basting the food and oiling the rack; heavy duty oven gloves; a bucket of water in case a flare-up gets out of control; and a metal brush for cleaning the rack between courses.

It is impossible to give exact cooking times because there are so many variables in open cooking – the heat of the coals, how close the rack is to them, the thickness of the food, and even the weather. If you are a beginner, I recommend you follow the recipe instructions exactly, keep a close watch on the food while it cooks, and keep testing until it is done to your liking – rare, medium or well done.

Trim the meats of excess fat so they won't cause flare-ups. Remember to follow the recipes as to how many times to turn the meat. Do not pour lots of marinade over food while it is cooking – always brush it on.

Aromatics are a final refinement to open cooking. Thrown on the coals towards the last minutes of cooking time, their perfume pervades the air and the food wonderfully. Use any type of fresh herb – it is worthwhile experimenting with different flavors. Hickory chips soaked in water enhance beef, chicken and duck. I like to toss a few eucalyptus leaves in the fire sometimes. Vine prunings are excellent for any type of food and you can also try garlic, orange peel, pine needles, bay leaves and fruit wood.

Marinades are essential to keep the food moist and impregnated with flavors against the fierce heat of the coals. The longer you marinate, the more tender the food will be – 24 or 48 hours will improve your chances of success as a barbecue cook. Never marinate for less than 2 hours. Take the food out of the refrigerator for an hour or two to allow it to reach room temperature before cooking.

Marinades are usually made up of a mixture of any of the following ingredients: oil, lemon, vinegar, beer, wine, soy sauce, alcohol, yogurt, honey, herbs, spices, onions, garlic and ginger. Experiment with the marinades in this book. For instance, use a lamb marinade with chicken instead–there are endless variations. When marinating, remember to turn the food occasionally in the bowl.

Baste the food as it cooks with the leftover marinade to prevent drying out. Sometimes lean meats are wrapped in fatty bacon or caul as a protection. For thousands of years, food has been wrapped in leaves such as banana and vine and cooked in the ashes of the fire. If you can get the fresh leaves, do use them. Scald them in boiling water for a minute first to make them more pliable. Otherwise, use a double layer of baking foil or greased parchment paper. Don't wrap the parcels up too tightly, as the food inside will be steaming and will create some nice juices.

The smoky herb flavor of barbecued food can be accentuated by strongly flavored sauces, such as chili and tomato sauce and aïoli. Sometimes you can use the marinade as a sauce as well, or the sauce as a marinade.

Do not be daunted by this long list of instructions – basically you are just throwing a piece of food on the fire and cooking it by the oldest method known. Even charred and overcooked steak can taste like the best steak you ever ate, in the relaxed atmosphere of a barbecue on a happy day. Cover it up with some homemade sauce and your friends may never notice. Keep practising!

# STARTERS & DRINKS

## Crudités with Vinaigrette

A popular way to begin a barbecue meal. Crudités are bite-sized pieces of raw vegetable for dipping in a sauce or dressing of your choice. Instead of vinaigrette, you could use any of the sauces in the next 4 recipes. The sauces also taste excellent with many of the meat and fish dishes in this book.

|   | |
|---|---|
|   | A bunch of spinach |
| 2 | heads of endive |
| 1 | fennel bulb |
| 6 | celery stalks |
| 6 | carrots |
| 2 | red sweet peppers |

FOR THE VINAIGRETTE
|   | |
|---|---|
|   | Salt and pepper |
| 1 | tablespoon Dijon mustard |
| 2 | tablespoons lemon juice |
| 6 | tablespoons cold-pressed virgin olive oil |

Wash and dry all the vegetables. Arrange the spinach leaves on a large plate as the base for the crudités. Tear the largest leaves, if necessary, to fit. Separate the leaves of the endive, thinly slice the fennel, cut the celery into suitable lengths and slice the carrots and the sweet peppers into julienne strips. Arrange attractively on the plate.

Make the vinaigrette by combining the salt, pepper, mustard, lemon juice and oil in a screw-top jar. Shake well and keep very cold before serving. To serve, pour the vinaigrette into individual bowls for the guests to dip the vegetables in.

VARIATIONS: Other vegetables to include in the crudités are small leaves of lettuce, tomatoes, beans, cucumbers, cabbage, cauliflower, avocado, beets, asparagus, radishes, celeriac, cooked potatoes and mushrooms and you can add hard-cooked eggs.

## Chili & Tomato Sauce

|   | |
|---|---|
| 2 | chilies |
| 2 | large tomatoes |
| 3 | garlic cloves |
| 1/4 | cup pine nuts |
| 3 | tablespoons lemon juice |
| 1 | cup oil |
|   | Salt and pepper |

Put the chilies, tomatoes, garlic and pine nuts in a oven at 350°F. Remove each as soon as it is cooked. Peel the tomatoes and garlic. Blend them all in a food processor. Gradually beat in the lemon juice and oil. Add salt and pepper.

## Aïoli

A garlic mayonnaise from the south of France. It goes very well with all types of seafood.

|   | |
|---|---|
| 6 | garlic cloves |
| 2 | egg yolks |
| 2 | teaspoons Dijon mustard |
| 1/2 | teaspoon salt |
| 1 | cup olive oil |
| 1 | tablespoon lemon juice |

Crush the garlic, peel and chop finely. Put the garlic, egg, mustard and salt into a bowl and beat. Slowly add the oil, drop by drop, until it emulsifies, then you can add it faster. When all the oil is mixed, stir the lemon juice in with a wooden spoon. Keep refrigerated until serving.

## Garlic Sauce

6 slices of white bread, crusts removed
6 garlic cloves, crushed
2 tablespoons lemon juice
1/2 cup olive oil
Water to measure
1/2 teaspoon salt
1 teaspoon pepper

Soak the bread in water and squeeze to remove excess. Put the bread, garlic and lemon juice into a food processor and blend. Gradually add the olive oil until the sauce resembles thick cream. Stir in water to thin the sauce a little and season with salt and pepper.

## Tarator Sauce

A slice of white bread
2 garlic cloves, crushed
1 cup walnut kernels
Salt
2/3 cup chicken stock
2 tablespoons lemon juice

Soak the bread in water and squeeze to remove excess. Blend the garlic, walnuts, bread and salt in a food processor. Slowly add the stock and then the lemon juice until the mixture is thick and smooth like a mayonnaise.

## Eggplant Salad

Serve this delicious salad with crudités or new bread. It can also be used as a sauce with roast or broiled lamb.

4 eggplants
1/3 cup lemon juice
1/3 cup olive oil
Salt
4 tablespoons unflavored yogurt

FOR THE GARNISH
12 black olives
2 tablespoons chopped parsley or mint

Cut the eggplants in half and place on a greased baking sheet. Bake in a preheated oven (400°F) for about 45 minutes or until soft. The skin is easily removed when still hot. Put the pulp into a food processor with the lemon juice, oil, salt and yogurt. Blend to a smooth paste. Serve in a shallow dish with the olives around the edge and sprinkle with the parsley or mint.

## Olivade

A very tasty starter to an outdoor meal. Simply spread some over a crust of new bread.

1 1/2 cups fromage frais or quark
1 pound black olives, pitted
4 tablespoons brandy

If you cannot get fromage frais or quark, blend cottage cheese in a food processor with 2 teaspoons of milk. Put all the ingredients into a food processor and blend to a smooth paste.

COOK'S NOTES: Have plenty of hearty starters ready for your guests to nibble at so they do not get too ravenous with the heady aromas issuing from the barbecue fire.

COOK'S NOTES: The recipes in this book will work just as well in the oven, under the broiler or on a griddle, when it isn't convenient to light the barbecue.

*Crudités served with tarator sauce. This sauce is very easy to make and is a nice change for a starter. It is very popular in the Middle East and can be used as a sauce with fish and poultry as well.*

*COOK'S NOTES: Marinate the food and make the sauces the day before the barbecue to insure a relaxed day for the cook.*

## Oysters in the Shell

Have everything ready before you put the oysters on the grill. Serve with wholewheat bread.

> *Oysters in their shells, 8 per person*
> *Salt*
> *Pepper*
> *Lemon wedges*
> *Chili and tomato sauce (p. 9)*

Place the oysters on the barbecue and grill for 6 minutes. Put straight onto plates with salt, pepper, lemon wedges and individual bowls of the chili and tomato sauce.

## Carrot & Potato Dip

*Carrot and potato dip is a hearty starter to a barbecue meal. It will keep your guests happy until the first barbecued treat is ready.*

Serve this spicy dip with fresh crusty bread or pita bread.

| | |
|---|---|
| 1 1/2 | pounds carrots, chopped |
| 1 | pound potatoes, chopped |
| 1/2 | teaspoon salt |
| 3 | garlic cloves, chopped |
| 4 | teaspoons cumin seeds |
| 1 | chili, chopped |
| 2 | tablespoons lemon juice |
| 3 | tablespoons olive oil |

Boil the carrots, potatoes and salt in water until the vegetables are soft. Drain and blend in a food processor with the garlic, cumin, chili and lemon juice. Gradually add the oil and blend to a smooth, thick consistency.

 COOK'S NOTES: Do not crowd the food too closely together on the grill – air needs to circulate around it.

## Cold Yogurt Soup

A cooling soup for a hot summer's day. Serve in mugs while everyone stands around the barbecue watching the main course cook. Add more water to turn it into a refreshing drink.

| | |
|---|---|
| 3 | cups unflavored yogurt |
| 1 | cup heavy cream |
| 1 | cup water |
| 1/2 | teaspoon salt, and pepper to taste |
| 2 | cups cucumber, peeled and chopped |
| 1/2 | cup mint leaves, finely chopped |

Combine all the ingredients in a bowl and mix well. Cover and keep refrigerated. serve in chilled mugs.

## Mozzarella & Bread Skewers

A simple and delicious barbecued dish from Italy that has been enjoyed for centuries.

| | |
|---|---|
| 1 | pound mozzarella cheese, cut into 1-inch cubes |
| | White bread, cut into 1-inch cubes, 6 more than the cheese |
| | Salt and pepper |
| 2/3 | cup butter |
| 4 | anchovy fillets, chopped |

*Cold yogurt soup is simple and fast to make. Leave out the cream if you prefer and add an extra cup of low-fat yogurt.*

Thread the cheese and bread onto the skewers alternately, starting and ending with bread. Sprinkle with salt and pepper. Melt a quarter of the butter and brush over the skewers. Place on the oiled grill, turning form time to time, until the bread and cheese are golden-brown.

In the meantime, melt the remaining butter and add the chopped anchovies. Serve with the anchovy butter poured over the skewers.

## Damper

The well-known Australian bushman's bread. Fun to make if you are having a barbecue. Bake in hot coals or cook it in a covered barbecue or an oven. Serve with Australian billy tea. To make billy tea, fill a billy can, or small lidded can, almost full with water. Add tea and 2 eucalyptus leaves. Put the lid on tightly and place the can over the heat. When it comes to a boil lift it off the heat, swing the billy twice over your head and the tea is ready to drink. A time-honored ritual.

| 3 | cups flour |
| 1 | tablespoon butter |
| 6 | teaspoons baking powder |
| | Salt |
| | Water |

In a bowl, mix the flour, butter, baking powder and salt together, using your fingertips, until it is the texture of bread crumbs. Make a well in the center and add a little water. Mix into the flour and keep adding water until it is a firm dough. Shape into a round loaf and put into the hot coals, making sure to have enough coals to put over the top as well. It will take about 45 minutes to cook. It is ready when the base is firm when tapped.

If cooking in the oven, preheat the oven at 400°F and bake for 45-60 minutes. In a covered barbecue it will take about 10 minutes less, depending on the heat of your fire.

*VARIATIONS: Add chopped herbs to the mixture or use wholemeal flour, and milk instead of water. A handful or two of chopped dried fruit makes a sweet addition.*

## Bruschetta

Another rustic Italian meal. Have the condiments ready before you toast the bread so you can eat it piping hot.

| 1 | loaf of crusty bread |
| 6 | garlic cloves, crushed |
| | Salt and pepper |
| 2 | tablespoons olive oil |

Cut the bread into thick slices and toast on both sides to a golden-brown. Rub each slice with a garlic clove. Sprinkle with salt and pepper and brush on the olive oil.

*VARIATION: Add a slice of prosciutto, quickly grilled, and a squeeze of lemon juice to each slice of bread.*

## Mulled Wine

| 2 | apples |
| | Juice of 1 lemon |
| 2 | bottles of red wine |
| 1 | teaspoon ground allspice |
| 3 | cinnamon sticks |
| 6 | whole cloves |
| 1/4 | cup superfine sugar |

Leave the peel on the apples and simply slice each one into four rings. Place immediately in water with the lemon juice and leave to soak for 15 minutes. Drain and combine the apple slices with the remaining ingredients in a saucepan. Heat up on the barbecue until almost boiling. Ladle into cups or mugs.

*Damper is an easy loaf to cook even if you are not an experienced breadmaker.*

## Orange Granita

A fresh refreshing drink for a summer's day barbecue. Have the frozen granita, the chilled glasses, and the guests ready at the same time so the granitas can be served immediately. Lemons, limes and grapefruit taste delicious prepared in the same way.

2     *cups granulated sugar*
4     *cups water*
       *Zest of 1 orange*
1 1/2 *cups orange juice*
6     *thin orange slices*

Dissolve the sugar in the water and bring it slowly to a boil. Add the zest. When it has boiled for a few minutes, remove from heat. Stir in the juice, strain and pour into ice-cube trays. Freeze for 12 hours.

To serve, crush ice-cubes in a food processor, about five at a time, until evenly crushed. Pour the granita straight into chilled tall glasses and garnish with a slice of orange.

# MEATS

## Lamb with Thyme & Garlic

A leg of lamb
A handful of thyme
Pepper
2  tablespoons olive oil
1  baked garlic head per person (p. 42)

Mix the thyme, pepper and olive oil together and rub over the lamb the same way as in the next recipe. Cook in a very hot covered barbecue or oven about 450°F, for 1 hour. Rest for 30 minutes in a warm place before carving. Serve with garlic heads, roast potatoes and pumpkin.

*Spicy Moroccan leg of lamb served with apricot sauce. Baked eggplant (p. 42) is being cooked with it to serve as a starter.*

## Moroccan Leg of Lamb

Moroccan lamb is cooked for a long time on a very low heat, so don't build up a roaring fire. It has to be cooked in a covered barbecue or oven at about 375°F. Serve with roast potatoes, apricot sauce and a sprinkling of cumin seeds.

*A leg of lamb*

FOR THE MARINADE
| | |
|---|---|
| 1 | tablespoon paprika |
| 1 | tablespoon ground cumin |
| 1/2 | cup mint leaves |
| 6 | garlic cloves, crushed |
| 2 | tablespoons grated ginger root |
| 1/2 | cup olive oil |

FOR THE GARNISH
Cumin seeds

FOR THE SAUCE
| | |
|---|---|
| 2/3 | cup dried apricots |
| 1 | teaspoon cinnamon |
| 2 | cups water |

Mix together the paprika, cumin, mint, garlic, ginger and olive oil. Rub the mixture all over the lamb. Loosen the flesh around the leg bone and slip some of the spice mixture into the space. Loosen the outside skin and slip some of the spice mixture between the skin and the flesh. Tie up the leg with string. Cook for up to 2 hours or until the meat is so soft and tender you could take it off with a spoon.

In the meantime, make the sauce by simmering the apricots and cinnamon in the water for about 30 minutes, or until they are soft. Blend in a food processor.

## Butterflied Leg of Lamb

A really spicy, but not too hot, Indian way of cooking lamb. Serve with rice, salad and chutney. Ask a butcher to bone the leg and butterfly it, which means cutting slashes into the solid meat so it is flattened out and all one thickness.

*A leg of lamb, butterflied*

FOR THE MARINADE
| | |
|---|---|
| 1 | onion, chopped |
| 1 1/2 | tablespoons chopped ginger root |
| 6 | garlic cloves, chopped |
| 2/3 | cup lemon juice |
| 1 | tablespoon ground coriander |
| 2 | tablespoons garam masala (p. 31) |
| 1 | tablespoon turmeric |
| 3 | chilies, chopped |
| 1 | cup olive oil |
| | Salt and pepper |

Trim the lamb of all the fat and put into a shallow dish. Put the onion, ginger, garlic, lemon juice, coriander, garam masala, turmeric and chilies into a food processor and blend to a smooth paste. Spread the paste over the lamb and rub it into the flesh, cutting a few pockets to allow the flavoring to penetrate the lamb. Cover and refrigerate, preferably for 24 hours.

Take the lamb out of the refrigerator 2 hours before barbecuing. If barbecued with a lid on, it will take 45-50 minutes. It will take a little longer if cooked like a steak. Brush the lamb with the marinade at least four times while it is cooking. Let the lamb rest for 20 minutes on a warmed plate before carving.

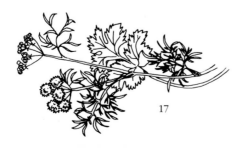

17

## Lamb Chops, Tandoori Style

Another Indian method of cooking. Serve with roast potatoes and a green salad.

12    *thick lamb loin chops*

*FOR THE MARINADE*
1    *tablespoon oil*
1    *tablespoon black peppercorns*
6    *whole cloves*
2    *bay leaves*
1    *tablespoon cardamom pods*
2    *cinnamon sticks*
2    *chilies*
1    *cup unflavored yogurt*
1    *tablespoon grated ginger root*
3    *garlic cloves, chopped*
1    *cup cilantro or mint leaves, chopped*
1/2    *teaspoon salt*

Heat the oil and fry the peppercorns, cloves, bay leaves, cardamom, cinnamon and chilies until the bay leaves begin to get darker.

Remove from heat and drain off the oil. Stir the spices into the yogurt along with the ginger, garlic, cilantro and salt. Mix well and pour over the chops which have been trimmed of excess fat. Leave to marinate for a few hours, unrefrigerated, and then cook over the barbecue fire. How long they take will depend on the thickness of the chops and whether you like them pink or well done.

## Roast Sirloin

This is suitable to cook on a spit, if you have one, or a covered barbecue. Serve with horseradish, mustard or chili and tomato sauce (p. 9).

3    *pounds sirloin roast*

*FOR THE MARINADE*
1/2    *cup butter, melted*
1    *teaspoon salt*
2    *tablespoons olive oil*
1    *tablespoon lemon juice*
1/3    *cup oregano*
3    *onions, chopped*
2    *teaspoons pepper*

Mix the oil, lemon juice, oregano, onion and pepper together and rub all over the beef. Cover and leave to marinate unrefrigerated, for 3 hours.

If using a spit, fix the meat on the spit and cook for 35-50 minutes, depending on the size of the roast and how well done you like it. Brush with melted butter every 10 minutes. If using a covered barbecue, place the meat on the grill and brush with butter three times during cooking. It will take the same time as spit roasting. Leave to rest for 20 minutes ,then sprinkle with salt just before serving.

*Roast sirloin ready to carve for the guests. It has rested for 20 minutes in a warm place to give the muscles time to relax so the meat is tender.*

---

## Barbecue Sauce

*Rosemary veal chops with a selection of barbecued vegetables (p. 40).*

This sauce is quick and easy to make and will store well in the refrigerator. As well as making an excellent sauce for steaks, it is delicious with fish, poultry, pork and lamb.

| | |
|---|---|
| 1/2 | cup olive oil |
| 3 | onions, chopped |
| 1 | cup tomato paste |
| 1/2 | cup wine vinegar |
| 1/2 | cup white wine |
| 1/2 | cup Worcestershire sauce |
| 2 | teaspoons thyme |
| 2 | garlic cloves, crushed |
| 4 | tablespoons clear honey |
| 2 | teaspoons Dijon mustard |
| | Salt and pepper |

Heat the oil and cook the onions until transparent. Add the tomato paste, vinegar, wine, Worcestershire sauce, thyme, garlic, honey and mustard. Mix well and cook, stirring constantly until the mixture is smooth and creamy. Season with salt and pepper to taste.

 *COOK'S NOTES: Barbecued steaks and chops should be crisp on the outside and juicy and pink inside. To achieve this, the surfaces of the meat should be sealed within the first few minutes over the hottest heat and then the meat cooked through over a lesser heat. Leave to rest in a warm place after cooking for the tenderest result.*

## Rosemary Veal Chops

These chops are very good if you cook them so they are a bit pink inside. Pepper and salt and a squeeze of lemon are all you need as condiments. Serve with a spinach and bacon salad.

6     large thick veal chops

FOR THE MARINADE
2     tablespoons olive oil
1     tablespoon sherry
5     garlic cloves, crushed
      Pepper
1/2   cup rosemary

Mix the marinade ingredients together. Trim the chops and pour the marinade over. Leave for 5 hours. Put the chops onto a well-oiled grill. Turn after 2 minutes and brush with marinade. Turn three times during cooking and keep basting. Just before taking from heat, throw some rosemary into the fire.

## Beef Steaks

It is important to trim the steaks so the fat doesn't cause flare-ups in the hot coals. Throw some herbs into the fire toward the end of the cooking to add fragrance to the meat. Serve with barbecue sauce (p. 20).

6     steaks, fillet or sirloin, 1½-inches thick

FOR THE MARINADE
1     cup olive oil
1     tablespoon lemon juice
4     garlic cloves, crushed
      Pepper

Trim the excess fat from the steaks. Mix together all the other ingredients and rub into the meat. Cover and leave to marinate for 2-3 hours unrefrigerated. Lay steaks on a well-oiled grill

and brush with marinade. Turn after 1 minute, without piercing the meat. Continually baste the steaks while they are cooking. Test with a sharp knife for preferred degree of rareness. Do not turn more than three times. Only add salt after the meat is cooked, as the salt would dry out the flesh during cooking.

VARIATION
PEPPER STEAK: Add 1/2 cup crushed black peppercorns to the above marinade and press in on both sides of the beef. Just before serving, warm 1/2 cup cognac in a small pan. Ignite it and pour, flaming, over the steaks.

 COOK'S NOTES: To check if steaks and chops are ready, press the surface of the meat with a spatula. If it is soft, the meat is rare; if springy, medium; and if stiff, well done. Otherwise, cut through a section of meat: if the juice is red, the meat is rare; if pink, medium; and if clear, well done.

## Beef Teriyaki

6     minute steaks

FOR THE MARINADE
1     garlic clove, chopped
1/2   teaspoon superfine sugar
1     teaspoon grated ginger root
1/2   cup soy sauce
1/2   cup mirin or dry sherry

Mix the garlic, sugar, ginger, soy sauce and mirin together and marinate meat for 1 hour. Proceed as for the beef steaks recipe above. Mix the remaining marinade with 1/2 cup of water and a teaspoon of sugar. Heat and pour over the steaks when serving.

## Barbecued Spareribs

A Chinese country-style dish. Serve with a rice salad and roasted corn. Sprinkle with five-spice powder when serving.

3    *pounds lean pork spareribs,*
      *cut in half and bones cut*

FOR THE MARINADE
1/2  *cup hoisin sauce*
1/3  *cup sugar*
1/3  *cup rice wine or dry sherry*
1    *teaspoon Chinese five-spice powder*

Trim the spareribs of excess fat. Combine the marinade ingredients and marinate the spareribs in the refrigerator for 4 hours. Put the spareribs onto an oiled grill and baste with the marinade when you turn them every 10 minutes. They should take 30-40 minutes to cook.

## Five-Spice Powder

Make your own five-spice mixture. It is infinitely superior to the bought product and has the most wonderful aroma. Grind together 1 tablespoon each of Szechuan pepper, fennel seeds, cloves, cinnamon and star anise.

## Vietnamese Spareribs

For variety use this marinade instead of the Chinese one. Cook in the same way as for barbecued spareribs and sprinkle cilantro or mint leaves over the ribs when serving.

1    *onion, chopped*
3    *garlic cloves, chopped*
2    *tablespoons superfine sugar*
2    *tablespoons Vietnamese fish sauce*
1    *teaspoon pepper*

Blend all the ingredients in a food processor and pour over the spareribs.

 *COOK'S NOTES: When cooking boneless roasts such as fillet of beef or loin of pork, treat them the same way as steaks–seal the surface in the first few minutes, then cook to rare, medium or well done.*

## Country-Style Pork Chops

Fruit is wonderful with pork, so make fruit sauce, if you have time. Otherwise serve with barbecue sauce (p.20), mustard or fruit kebabs.

6    *thick pork chops*

FOR THE MARINADE
1/2  *cup olive oil*
1/3  *cup vinegar*
2    *garlic cloves, chopped*
1    *tablespoon thyme*
1    *teaspoon pepper*
2    *tablespoons Dijon mustard*

Combine all the marinade ingredients and pour over the chops. Cover and marinate for 12 hours in the refrigerator. Remove for 1 hour before cooking. Place the chops on a well-oiled grill and cook for about 15 minutes, turning three times and basting with marinade.

## Fruit Sauce

1/2    cup dried figs
1/2    cup raisins
1/2    cup prunes
1 1/2  cups water
1/2    cup brandy
1      tablespoon grated ginger root

Soak the dried fruits in the water and brandy for 30 minutes. Add the ginger and cook slowly for about 15 minutes, or until soft. Purée the sauce in the food processor. Serve warm.

## Mixed Grill & Kebabs

Many cuisines have a version of the mixed grill. A selection of meats allows guests to choose and compare flavors. The meats are cut to bite-sized pieces, marinated and cooked on skewers. You can include different types of sausage, pieces of chicken, kidneys, liver and chops, all marinated in the same mixture.

## Italian Mixed Grill

1    pound boneless chicken meat
1    pound boneless lamb shoulder
1    pound boneless pork
1    pound lamb's liver
     Sage leaves

FOR THE MARINADE
1/2  cup olive oil
2    tablespoons lemon juice
1/3  cup rosemary
1    tablespoon pepper

Cut meat into bite-sized pieces. Mix the marinade ingredients and pour over the meats. Marinate for 2 hours unrefrigerated.

Thread the meats on skewers with a sage leaf between each piece. Mix the meats or skewer them separately. Cook on an oiled grill for up to 10 minutes, basting constantly.

## Indian Lamb Kebabs

The lamb should marinate for 12-24 hours for the tenderest result. Remove from refrigerator an hour before cooking. Serve with rice and a salad.

1    leg or 2 shoulders of lamb

FOR THE MARINADE
1/3  cup tomato paste
1    cup yogurt
1    tablespoon dry mustard
2    tablespoons oil
4    tablespoons lemon juice
4    tablespoons garam masala (p. 31)
8    garlic cloves, chopped
1    tablespoon chopped ginger root
5    chilies, chopped

Cut the meat into bite-sized pieces, trimming off all the fat. Put all the marinade ingredients into a food processor and blend to a paste. Put the meat into the marinade, cover and refrigerate for at least 4 hours.

Thread the meat on skewers and keep in the marinade until ready to cook. Cook for about 10 minutes on an oiled grill, basting constantly. Sprinkle with fresh cilantro or mint leaves before serving.

*Overleaf: Delicious sweet orange granitas (p.15) makes a perfect drink for a summer barbecue.*

23

## Souvlakia or Greek Kebabs

2      shoulders of lamb
2      onions
20    bay leaves

FOR THE MARINADE
1/2   cup olive oil
1/3   cup lemon juice
1/3   cup chopped oregano
6      garlic cloves, chopped
       Pepper

Cut shoulders into bite-sized pieces, trimmed of fat. Mix all the marinade ingredients together and marinate meat for at least 2 hours.

Peel the onions, cut in half and gently prize the layers apart. Break the bay leaves into two. Thread the meat pieces on skewers, alternating meat, onion and bay leaf. Cook on an oiled grill for up to 10 minutes, basting and turning.

## Hamburgers

Everybody's favorite–and what a different flavor a homemade hamburger has. Serve in pita bread as a change from buns.

2      pounds lean ground beef
1      onion, finely chopped
2      garlic cloves, chopped
1      teaspoon salt
1      teaspoon pepper
1      teaspoon Worcestershire sauce
3      eggs
1      tablespoon parsley
1      teaspoon thyme

Combine all the ingredients thoroughly. Form into six hamburgers. Refrigerate until ready to cook. Cook for about 5 minutes on each side.

VARIATION: Add 2/3 cup black olives, pitted and finely chopped. Serve with a slice of ricotta cheese, chili and tomato sauce (p. 9).

## Quail & Liver Skewers

Spectacular-looking kebabs to delight your friends. Serve with pita bread and baked tomatoes (p. 42).

3      slices of pork liver
6      quail
6      slices of prosciutto
6      sausages
6      slices of bread
12    bay leaves

FOR THE MARINADE
1      tablespoon rosemary
       Olive oil
       Juice of 1 lemon

Cut the meats and bread into bite-sized pieces. Combine all the marinade ingredients. Thread the meats, bread pieces and bay leaves onto skewers in this order–sausage, bread, bay leaf, liver, quail, liver, bay leaf, bread, sausage. Pour the marinade over and leave to stand, covered, for 2 hours. Cook on an oiled grill for up to 10 minutes, basting constantly until they are pink or well done, as preferred.

 COOK'S NOTES: When making satays, be sure to soak the bamboo skewers in water first for an hour so they won't catch on fire. Thread them just before cooking.

I find that shoulder of lamb is the tenderest meat for Greek kebabs. Serve with rice salad or jacket potatoes.

## Spicy Sausages

Spicy yogurt salad (p. 43) would be a fine accompaniment to this dish along with potatoes baked in their jackets.

| | |
|---|---|
| 2 | pounds ground pork and veal |
| 1 | tablespoon ground coriander seeds |
| 1 | tablespoon ground cumin seeds |
| 1 | teaspoon ground cinnamon |
| 1 | teaspoon pepper |
| 1/2 | teaspoon ground cloves |
| 1 | teaspoon salt |
| 3 | tablespoons lemon juice |
| | Sausage skins, soaked in hot water |

Roast the coriander and cumin in a dry pan for 3 minutes. Put into a bowl with the meat, the other spices, salt and lemon juice. Mix together thoroughly. Wash the sausage skins under the tap, making sure they are open. Attach one end to a sausage funnel and force the meat mixture through, into the skins. Twist at intervals to make short or long sausages, as preferred. Prick them all over with a needle and store in the refrigerator until ready to cook. Cook on an oiled grill until nicely browned.

*VARIATION: For a spectacular effect, instead of making individual sausages, make a single long sausage, coil it, and barbecue it in one large ring.*

## Moroccan Brochettes

Many countries have different recipes for basically the same meatballs grilled on skewers over hot coals. Only the condiments change.

| | |
|---|---|
| 2 | pounds lamb, finely ground |
| 2 | onions, finely chopped |
| 1 | cup parsley, finely chopped |
| 1 | teaspoon ground cinnamon |
| 1 | teaspoon ground cumin |
| 1 | teaspoon ground coriander |
| 1 | teaspoon salt |
| 1 | tablespoon pepper |
| | Oil for basting |

Combine all the ingredients except the oil and mix thoroughly. Shape the meat like a flattened sausage around each skewer. Cook on an oiled grill turning only once. Brush with oil to prevent drying out. They should be ready in about 7 minutes. If you find the shape troublesome, roll them up into meatballs.

*VARIATION:*
*KOFTA: Indian meatballs on skewers. Make the same way as above, but replace the spices with 1 tablespoon garam masala (p. 31) and add 2 tablespoons unflavored yogurt and 1/2 teaspoon cayenne.*

 *COOK'S NOTES: Always oil the grill well so the food doesn't stick. Clean it with a wire brush in between courses and oil again.*

*Spicy sausages are a guaranteed success at any barbecue–there are never any left. If you are nervous about making sausages, or haven't the time, make the mixture into meatballs.*

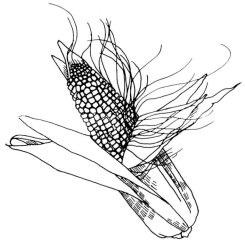

# POULTRY

## Tandoori Chicken

The chicken can be cooked whole in a covered barbecue or grilled, cut into 10 serving pieces. Indians usually remove the skin, but you may keep it on if you prefer. Plan to marinate for 24 hours if possible, as the marinade tenderizes the chicken wonderfully.

| | |
|---|---|
| 1 | large chicken or 2 small ones |

FOR THE MARINADE
| | |
|---|---|
| 1 | onion, chopped |
| 6 | garlic cloves, chopped |
| 2 | tablespoons chopped ginger root |
| 3 | tablespoons lemon juice |
| 2 | cups yogurt |
| 2 | tablespoons garam masala (p. 31) |
| 1 | teaspoon salt |
| 1 | teaspoon pepper |
| 1/2 | teaspoon cayenne |
| 1/2 | teaspoon Indian red food coloring, |

FOR THE GARNISH
| | |
|---|---|
| 6 | lemon wedges |
| | Cilantro leaves |

Cut up and skin the chicken, if desired. Slash the flesh so that the marinade can penetrate. Blend the onion, garlic, ginger and lemon juice to a smooth paste in a food processor. Pour into the marinating bowl and add the yogurt, garam masala, salt, pepper, cayenne, and food coloring, if wanted. Mix thoroughly, then add the chicken, rubbing the marinade into the chicken flesh.

Remove the chicken from the refrigerator 1 hour before cooking. Place on an oiled grill and either bake in a covered barbecue for approximately 40 minutes or, if cooking chicken pieces, grill for about 7 minutes each side. Check that chicken is cooked through and not pink. Remember to baste frequently. Serve garnished with lemon wedges and cilantro leaves.

## Coconut Chicken

These chicken pieces would originally have been wrapped in banana leaves. If you can get them, cut the leaves into squares and blanch them for a minute in boiling water. Otherwise, use two layers of foil.

| | |
|---|---|
| 3 | pounds chicken, cut into serving pieces |
| 1 | cup unsweetened creamed coconut |
| 1 | onion, chopped |
| 3 | garlic cloves |
| 1 | tablespoon chopped lemon grass |
| 1 | teaspoon turmeric |
| 1 | teaspoon salt |
| 2 | teaspoons pepper |

Trim the chicken of fat and skin. In a food processor, blend coconut, onion, garlic, lemon grass, turmeric, salt and pepper to a smooth paste. Marinate the chicken pieces for several hours, unrefrigerated. Securely wrap up each piece of chicken with some marinade in foil or, banana leaf. Cook on the barbecue for about 25 minutes.

 *COOK'S NOTES: Follow the recipe instructions for sealing the food. This is important to seal in the tasty juices that keep the food moist.*

# Mango Chicken

| 6 | chicken breasts |
| 4 | mangoes, peeled and sliced |
| 1 | teaspoon salt |
| 2 | teaspoons pepper |
| 1 | tablespoon garam masala |
| 1 | tablespoon tomato paste |
| 3 | onions, finely sliced |
| 1 | cup white wine |

Remove skin and fat from the chicken. Combine the remaining ingredients and mix well. Lay each chicken breast on a bed of the mango mixture and wrap up individually in foil or banana leaves. They will take about 25 minutes to cook on a hot grill. Be sure to serve with bread or rice to mop up the juices.

# Garam Masala

Homemade garam masala is far superior to the bought variety. Use good ingredients to start with and keep the spice in an airtight jar in the refrigerator and it will last for months.

| 1 | tablespoon cardamom seeds |
| 1 | tablespoon cumin seeds |
| 1 | teaspoon whole cloves |
| 1 | teaspoon black peppercorns |
| 1 | nutmeg |
| 1 | cinnamon stick |

Grind spices in a coffee grinder or food mill.

*Delicious spicy pieces of tandoori chicken, tenderized with yogurt. Serve with rice, chutney and yogurt salad.*

# Italian Grilled Chicken

I have allowed half a chicken per person; if you have large chickens, split each chicken in four. Throw some extra rosemary onto the fire just before the chicken has finished cooking.

3    small chickens
12   lemon wedges

FOR THE MARINADE
2/3  cup lemon juice
2/3  cup olive oil
1    tablespoon pepper
1/2  cup rosemary

Split each chicken by laying it breast down and cutting it open right along the backbone. Crack the breastbone with a large sharp knife and arrange the chicken so it is as flat as possible. Cut into the wing and leg joints a little to flatten them. Turn the chicken over and flatten the inside as much as possible. Remove any fat and trim off the end of the wings.

Combine the marinade ingredients and marinate the chicken for 4 hours. Put the chicken on a well-oiled grill, skin-side down first. Turn over onto the carcass side after about 15 minutes. Baste all through the cooking process and turn three times. Grill until the skin side is golden-brown, about an hour altogether. Serve with lemon wedges and roast potatoes.

# Glazed Chicken wings

Honey and lime combine to keep the chicken succulent and moist. This recipe works just as well with the breast or thighs of a chicken.

18   chicken wings
     Hickory chips, soaked in water
12   lime wedges

FOR THE MARINADE
1/2  cup oil
3/4  cup white wine
1/3  cup lime juice
3    tablespoons thin honey
1    onion, finely chopped
2    tablespoons marjoram
1    teaspoon salt
2    teaspoons pepper

Trim the chicken wings, wash and dry. Mix all the marinade ingredients together and marinate the chicken wings for 12 hours. Take out of the refrigerator an hour before cooking time. Place on a well-oiled grill and brush with marinade frequently while grilling. They should take about 20 minutes. Throw some hickory chips into the fire half-way through cooking if you like, to give a more aromatic and smoky taste. Serve with lime wedges.

*The wonderful aromatic flavor of rosemary pervades Italian grilled chicken.*

## Japanese Chicken Kebabs

| | |
|---|---|
| 1 | chicken |
| 1 | cup chicken livers |
| 3 | red sweet peppers |

FOR THE MARINADE

| | |
|---|---|
| 1/2 | cup soy sauce |
| 1/2 | cup cup mirin or dry sherry |
| 1/3 | cup oil |
| 1 | tablespoon superfine sugar |
| 3 | garlic cloves, chopped |
| | Grated peel of 1 orange |

Cut the chicken into bite-sized pieces then trim off fat and skin. Trim chicken livers and cut into bite-size pieces. Core the sweet peppers and cut into squares. Mix the marinade ingredients together and pour over the chicken and livers. Leave to marinate in the refrigerator for several hours.

Thread on small skewers, alternating chicken pieces, liver and sweet pepper. Cook for 8-10 minutes on an oiled grill, brushing frequently with the marinade.

## Spicy Duck

Ducks have a heavy frame and a high fat content; you will need half a duck per person

| | |
|---|---|
| 3 x | 3-pound ducks |

FOR THE MARINADE

| | |
|---|---|
| 1 | cup fine cut orange marmalade |
| 1/2 | cup red wine vinegar |
| 1 | tablespoon Dijon mustard |
| 1 | tablespoon pepper |
| 1 | onion, finely sliced |

Split the ducks in half lengthways, through the backbone, try to flatten out as much as possible. Trim off extraneous fat and cut off the wing tips. Mix marinade ingredients together and pour over the ducks. Leave to marinate for 2 hours.

Grill the ducks on an oiled grill, skin-side down for 20 minutes. Turn and grill for a further 25 minutes or until they are well done and the skin is crisp. Brush with marinade three times during cooking. Brush the ducks with the remaining marinade before serving.

## Grilled Poussins

I have allowed one poussin per person. This recipe works beautifully with quail also–allow two per person and they will only take 5-6 minutes to cook.

| | |
|---|---|
| 6 | poussins |
| 1/2 | cup butter melted |
| 1 | teaspoon salt |
| 1 | cup cilantro leaves, chopped |

FOR THE MARINADE

| | |
|---|---|
| 1 | cup olive oil |
| 6 | garlic cloves, crushed |
| 2 | tablespoons paprika |
| 1 | tablespoon ground cumin |
| 1/4 | teaspoon cayenne |
| 1 | tablespoon pepper |

Split the poussin the same way as in the Italian grilled chicken (p. 33). Mix the marinade ingredients together and marinate the poussins for several hours. Place the birds on a well-oiled grill, skin-side down first. Add melted butter to the remaining marinade and baste the birds frequently. Turn three times. They will take 20-25 minutes to cook. Test by pricking the thigh to see if the juice is no longer pink. When cooked, sprinkle with salt and cilantro.

# FISH & SHELLFISH

## Lebanese Grilled Fish

I have allowed one fish per person. Any small fish, white or dark flesh, will be suitable for this pungent marinade. Serve with pita bread and tabbouleh (page 44).

| | |
|---|---|
| 6 | whole fish, cleaned and scaled |
| 1/3 | cup olive oil |
| 2 | onions, finely chopped |
| 3 | chilies, chopped |
| 1 | red sweet pepper, finely chopped |
| 6 | garlic cloves, chopped |
| 1 | cup mint leaves, chopped |
| 1/2 | cup slivered almonds |
| 1/2 | cup tahini |
| 1/3 | cup lemon juice |

To make the sauce, heat 1 tablespoon of oil in a pan and add the onions, chilies, sweet pepper, garlic and mint. Cook until they are soft, stirring constantly. Add half the almonds, stir for a minute, then remove from heat. Put the mixture into a food processor along with the tahini and lemon juice. Blend to a smooth sauce. Add the remaining almonds.

Brush the fish inside with some of the sauce, then brush the outside with oil. Place the fish on an oiled grill and cook for about 7 minutes on each side or until done. Serve the fish with the sauce poured over.

 COOK'S NOTES: Use a grilling rack for cooking small fish and fillets to save yourself the trouble of turning them. There are also grilling baskets for large fish but I don't think they are as necessary.

## Grilled Fish

A delicious, aromatic dish for a special occasion. This recipe is suitable for cooking a large fish with white flesh. Ask your fishmonger to clean and scale the fish for you. Serve it with tarator sauce (p. 10).

| | |
|---|---|
| 1 x | 3-pound firm white fish with head and tail left on A few branches of rosemary |
| 1/2 | cup flour |
| 1 | teaspoon salt |
| 2 | teaspoons pepper |
| 1 | tablespoon olive oil |
| 2 | tablespoons brandy Lemon wedges |

Stuff the fish with some of the rosemary. Roll the fish in flour, season with salt and pepper and sprinkle with olive oil. Tie some rosemary branches around the fish. Lay it on a hot, oiled grill and cook for 20-25 minutes, turning three times. Check it is cooked with the point of a knife – if the flesh flakes away, it is ready. It is better for fish to be slightly underdone than overdone and dry.

When ready, pour warm brandy over the fish and ignite. Bring the fish flaming to the table. Serve with lemon wedges.

## Snapper with Cilantro

One of my favorite methods of cooking fish. The fish remains moist and succulent–it is an almost fool proof recipe. The fish would have originally been cooked in a banana leaf but you can use 2 layers of foil instead.

| | |
|---|---|
| 1 | snapper or firm white fish, 2-pounds |
| 1 | tablespoon chopped ginger root |
| 6 | garlic cloves, chopped |
| 2 | chilies |
| 1 | tablespoon oil |
| 1 | teaspoon whole black mustard seeds |
| 1 | teaspoon cardamom seeds |
| 1 | teaspoon turmeric |
| 1 | cup cilantro, chopped |
| 1/3 | cup lime juice |

Ask your fish store to clean and scale the fish for you. Put the ginger, garlic and chili in a food processor with 2 tablespoons of water and blend to a smooth paste. Heat the oil in a pan and add the mustard and cardamom seeds. When they start to pop, pour in the ginger paste and the turmeric, stir and cook for a few minutes. Now return the mixture to the food processor, add the cilantro and lime juice and blend to a smooth paste.

The fish should be placed on a double layer of foil, and covered inside and out with the paste. Wrap the fish securely and put into a covered barbecue to cook for about 25 minutes. Serve with the paste and juices poured over each serving. These quantities serves 4.

 COOK'S NOTES: When buying fish and shell-fish, choose only the freshest ingredients. Whole fish should have bright eyes and shiny scales and skin. Fillets and steaks should be moist and glistening. Try to buy shellfish live.

## Seafood Kebabs

Add water-soaked hickory chips to the barbecue fire when cooking these kebabs to add a delicious smoky flavor to the seafood.

| | |
|---|---|
| 4 | salmon steaks, 1-inch thick |
| 4 | steaks of firm white fish, 1-inch thick |
| 12 | large shrimp in the shell |
| 24 | bottled mussels |

FOR THE MARINADE
| | |
|---|---|
| | Juice of 1 orange |
| | Juice of half a grapefruit |
| 1/2 | cup olive oil |
| 1 | tablespoon thin honey |
| 1 | tablespoon pepper |

Cut fish steaks into 1-inch cubes. Devein shrimp by running a knife along the back and pulling out the vein, leaving the whole shell on. Wash shrimp thoroughly. Mix marinade ingredients and pour over all the seafood. Leave to marinate in the refrigerator for 3 hours.

Arrange the seafood on skewers, alternating the two fish, shrimp and mussels. Cook the kebabs on an oiled grill for 10-15 minutes, brushing frequently with the marinade. Serve with garlic sauce (p. 10).

## Trout in Newspaper

The best trout I have ever tasted was one I caught myself and cooked in newspaper in the hot ashes of a rough camp fire. Any large fish could be cooked this way, either in hot ashes or over any barbecue.

| | |
|---|---|
| 1 x | 3-pound trout |
| 1 | tablespoon salt |
| | Lemon wedges |

Gut and wash the fish. Trout does not have scales but if the fish you have chosen does, the scales will peel off with the newspaper. Rub the salt inside the fish. Take ten large sheets of newspaper, wet them and use them to wrap the fish securely. Either bury the parcel in hot ashes for about 45 minutes or, if using an open barbecue, cook for about 1 hour, turning a few times. Remove the fish from the paper, leaving behind the skin and scales. Serve with lemon.

*Snapper with cilantro. The cilantro spice paste harmonizes well with the succulent coral snapper.*

## Barbecued Tuna Steaks

When choosing fish steaks, buy 1-inch thick steaks, so they will not dry out in cooking. Any large fish with firm flesh, like tuna, is suitable. Serve with a sauce such as chili and tomato sauce (p. 9), aïoli (p. 9), or tarator sauce (p. 10). Vary the herbs–thyme, fennel, tarragon and rosemary are wonderful as well.

6    *thick slices of fresh tuna, trimmed*
6    *lemon wedges*
*FOR THE MARINADE*
*1/2    cup oil*
*1/3    cup lemon juice*
*1/2    cup dill, chopped*
*2    garlic cloves*
*1    teaspoon pepper*

*Trout marinating before being put on the grill. I used the same marinade and method of barbecuing as for barbecued tuna steaks. Serve with roast potatoes and salad.*

Mix marinade ingredients together and pour over the fish steaks. Leave to marinate, refrigerated, for 2 hours. Cook fish on an oiled grill, turning three times and brushing with the marinade in between. Tuna is excellent a little underdone. Serve with lemon wedges and any of the sauces mentioned above.

## Grilled Lobster

A simple recipe for a luxurious treat. Lobster is so rich it does not need much embellishing. I have allowed half a lobster per person. The fresher the shellfish, the better it will taste.

3 x    1½-pound live lobsters
1      tablespoon pepper
1/2    cup butter, melted
12     lime wedges
       Sprigs of watercress

Wrap lobsters tightly in newspaper and place in the deep freeze for 30 minutes. This will quickly kill the lobsters, in the most humane way without freezing the meat. Cut the lobsters in half lengthways. Remove the intestines and the other matter, clean and wipe well. Stir the pepper into the melted butter and brush over the lobsters.

Place the lobsters, flesh-side down, on an oiled grill for 5 minutes. Turn over and cook for 10 more minutes, basting constantly with the butter. When cooked, serve garnished with lime wedges and sprigs of watercress.

## Barbecued Garlic Shrimp

Delicious garlicky shrimp. Serve with warm bread and salad.

3      pounds fresh large shrimp

FOR THE MARINADE
1/2    cup olive oil
1/3    cup lemon juice
1      onion, chopped
15     garlic cloves, chopped
1      tablespoon chopped ginger root
3      chilies, chopped
1      tablespoon pepper

FOR THE GARNISH
12     lemon wedges
2      tablespoons mint leaves

Devein the shrimp by cutting open the back and pulling out the veins. Clean thoroughly and wipe dry, leaving the whole shell on. Mix all the marinade ingredients together and blend in a food processor. Pour over the clean shrimp and marinate in the refrigerator for 2 hours. Place the shrimp on an oiled grill, baste, cook for 5 minutes, turn and cook a few more minutes and they should be done. Serve with lemon wedges and chopped mint.

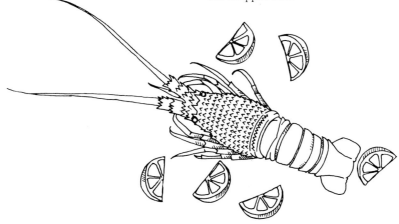

# VEGETABLES & SALADS

## Barbecued Vegetables

My favorite way of cooking vegetables such as potatoes, pumpkins, sweet potatoes, onions and turnips is to leave them whole in their skins, brush them with oil and bake them in a covered barbecue or in the ashes of an open fire. The smoke enhances the flavors. Usually the meat or fish dishes take time to prepare so I do not want to spend too much time on the vegetables–besides, barbecues are all about having a relaxing time!

Some people prefer to wrap the vegetables in foil, especially when cooking in the ashes. Brush the foil with melted butter or oil and season with salt, pepper, garlic or other herbs before wrapping up the packages.

**POTATOES** are excellent sprinkled with a teaspoon of caraway seeds or fennel seeds before being wrapped in buttered foil. Serve with extra butter. You could also insert a garlic clove in each potato. Cook sweet potatoes and yams the same way. They take 50-70 minutes, depending on their size and heat of the fire.

**CARROTS, TURNIPS and PARSNIPS** are wonderful lightly oiled and grilled over an open fire; or wrapped in buttered foil with a teaspoon of chopped dill and a pinch of pepper sprinkled over each one. Carrots and turnips take from 50 minutes but parsnips may take only 30 minutes.

**ONIONS** are best kept in their skins and taken out when they are cooked. They do not need foil. They take about 40 minutes to cook.

**CORN-ON-THE-COB**. Grill these over an open fire, brushing with butter as you turn them. Serve them with fresh lime juice and freshly ground pepper. If you can buy them in their husks, it is best to cook them that way. Gently pull down the husk, take off the silk, and soak the corn in water for 10 minutes to prevent the husks from burning. Dry, salt and pepper the corn, brush with olive oil or melted butter and bring the husk back over the corn. Tie up with string. They will take 20 minutes to cook.

**RED and GREEN SWEET PEPPERS**. Barbecue cooking is perfect for making a pepper salad. Cut them in half lengthwise and remove the seeds. Cook on the grill until the skin blisters and is slightly black. Peel the skin off and slice the sweet pepper. Serve with a vinaigrette dressing (page 9).

**MUSHROOMS** are excellent grilled on the barbecue, especially if you have just picked them yourself. Wipe them clean and trim the stalk. Brush with oil or melted butter and put on the oiled grill. Turn only once and baste again. Button mushrooms take 5-10 minutes, but huge field mushrooms could take up to 20 minutes.

**GARLIC**. In the South of France they bake whole heads of garlic to accompany meat and fish one head per person. It may sound excessive but it isn't, as the cooking transforms the garlic so it is mellow and creamy and not as pungent as raw garlic. I soak the heads in water before cooking so the outer leaves don't burn. They take about 30-40 minutes to cook.

**GLOBE ARTICHOKES** are delicious cooked on the grill or in a covered barbecue. Wash and trim them, then open up the leaves as far as possible. Sprinkle with salt and pour some olive oil and a squeeze of lemon over the leaves, making sure it gets down between them. They take about 30 minutes to cook.

*A selection of barbecued vegetables ready to serve with the main dish.*

## Baked Eggplant

3     medium size eggplant
      Salt
3     garlic cloves, chopped
1     tablespoon pepper
2     tablespoons mint
2     large tomatoes, thinly sliced
1/2   pound goat's cheese

Cut the eggplant in half lengthwise. Score the cut flesh and sprinkle with salt. Leave for 30 minutes, then wash and dry them. Sprinkle garlic, pepper and mint over the cut surfaces. Lay tomato slices, then slices of goat's cheese over the top. Cook in a covered barbecue for 45 minutes or until the eggplant is cooked and the cheese is melted and turning brown.

## Spicy Yogurt Salad

A very refreshing starter, or an accompaniment to a spicy meal. I sometimes have some for my lunch with pita bread.

4     large carrots, grated
1/2   cup walnuts chopped

FOR THE DRESSING
2     cups yogurt
      Juice of 1 lemon
3     garlic cloves, crushed
1/3   cup cilantro, chopped
1     chili, chopped
1     teaspoon ground cumin
1/2   teaspoon ground coriander
      Cilantro leaves

Combine all dressing ingredients and mix well. Add the carrots and walnuts. Sprinkle cilantro leaves over the surface when serving.

*VARIATIONS: Try a combination of tomatoes, basil and pine nuts for a change. Apple, mint and hazelnuts are excellent too.*

## Baked Ginger Pumpkin

These pumpkin halves taste delicious with grilled chicken, or they make a great starter to a hearty meal.

3     small butternut pumpkins
1     tablespoon oil
      Pepper
10    garlic cloves , chopped
3     tablespoons chopped ginger root

Cut pumpkins in half and remove the seeds. Wash the skin. Brush all over with oil. Mix the garlic and ginger together and place in the seed cavity. Sprinkle all over with pepper. Place in a covered barbecue or ashes, wrapped in foil. Cooking will take 50-60 minutes.

## Baked Tomatoes

Serve baked tomatoes as an accompaniment to meat and fish or as a starter.

6     large tomatoes
1     teaspoon salt
1/2   cup bread crumbs
6     garlic cloves, crushed
1     cup basil, finely chopped
2     teaspoons pepper
      Oil for brushing

Cut the tomatoes in half and sprinkle with salt. Mix together with bread crumbs, garlic, basil and pepper and press this mixture into the cut surface of the tomato. If necessary, scoop a little of the tomato out. Place on an oiled grill in a covered barbecue or wrap in foil and place in the ashes. They will take about 25 minutes to cook.

*Baked tomatoes filled with bread crumbs and basil.*

 *COOK'S NOTES: Place vegetables in a grilling rack to make them easier to turn and serve. Make sure all the pieces are the same thickness for even cooking.*

*Tabbouleh. A refreshing salad of parsley and mint for a summer barbecue.*

## Bean & Tomato Salad

A hearty Italian salad guaranteed to help curb the most voracious appetite.

| | |
|---|---|
| 1/2 | *pound dried cannellini beans* |
| 1/2 | *cup olive oil* |
| 5 | *garlic cloves, crushed* |
| 3 | *pounds tomatoes, chopped* |
| 12 | *large sage leaves* |
| 1 | *teaspoon salt* |
| | *Juice of 1 lemon* |

Soak the beans in water overnight. Drain and cover with fresh water. Put into a saucepan with half the oil and 6 sage leaves. Boil rapidly for 10 minutes and simmer until the beans are only just tender. Drain the beans.

Put the remaining oil and sage into a pan, add the garlic, beans, tomatoes and salt and cook for 10 minutes. Remove from heat. Pour the lemon juice over and mix the salad.

## Tabbouleh

| | |
|---|---|
| 3/4 | *cup cracked wheat* |
| 1/2 | *cup chopped scallions* |
| 2 | *tomatoes, finely chopped* |
| 1 1/2 | *cups parsley, chopped* |
| 1/2 | *cup mint, chopped* |

*FOR THE DRESSING*

| | |
|---|---|
| 3 | *tablespoons olive oil* |
| 1/2 | *cup lemon juice* |
| | *Salt and pepper to taste* |

Soak the cracked wheat for 30 minutes. Drain. Mix the dressing ingredients and pour over the wheat in a salad bowl. Leave to marinate for an hour. Add the scallions, tomatoes, parsley and mint to the bowl and toss gently.

# DESSERTS

## Summer Berries

Make this dessert just before serving. The berry fruits soften if left marinating too long.

| | |
|---|---|
| 1 | cup raspberries |
| 1 | cup strawberries |
| 1 | cup blueberries |
| 2 | teaspoons balsamic vinegar |
| 2 | tablespoons superfine sugar |

FOR THE DRESSING
| | |
|---|---|
| 1 | cup sour cream |
| 3 | tablespoons lime juice |
| 2 | tablespoons white rum |

Put the washed berries in a bowl and sprinkle vinegar and 1 tablespoon of sugar over them. Whip the sour cream with the lime juice and remaining sugar. Add the rum. When serving, arrange the berries and juice on a plate then place the lime dressing beside them.

## Fruit on Skewers

An attractive way to cook fruit on the barbecue, fruit skewers can accompany meat dishes or be eaten as a dessert. Fruits suitable for skewers are hard bananas, pineapples, pears, apples, peaches and nectarines.

## Chocolate Bananas

As children, we found this course the best part of a family barbecue. We always cooked the bananas in the ashes but it works just as well in a covered barbecue.

| | |
|---|---|
| 6 | large bananas |
| 3 | tablespoons melted chocolate |

Carefully slit the skins of the bananas lengthwise. Gently prize open and pour a tablespoon of chocolate in each. Fold the skins back and place bananas on the grill with the split sides uppermost. They should be cooked in 10-15 minutes, but it depends on the ripeness of the banana and the heat of the fire, so watch carefully.

VARIATION: Adults may pour a little dark rum inside the banana with the chocolate.

FOR THE MARINADE
| | |
|---|---|
| 1/2 | cup butter, melted |
| 1 | tablespoon dark brown sugar |
| 1 | teaspoon ground cinnamon |

Cut bite-sized pieces of fruit, soak in a mixture of 1 cup water to 2 tablespoons of lemon juice for 30 minutes. Thread fruit on skewers and brush with the marinade before and during cooking. This will caramelize the fruit over the fire. Serve the fruit skewers with some of the leftover marinade.

## Orange & Grapefruit Salad

A refreshing, tasty way to end a perfect meal

6     oranges
2     grapefruit
      Juice to measure
3     tablespoons thin honey
2     tablespoons orange blossom water
1/2   cup pistachio nuts, chopped

Cut the oranges and grapefruit into segments. The best method is to peel the fruit so there is no pith left, hold the orange in one hand with the top upward and, with a very sharp knife, cut between each segment so you avoid the skin that binds it. Squeeze leftover pulp when finished to extract the juice. Put segments into a bowl. Mix together the extracted juice, honey and orange blossom water. When the honey is dissolved, pour over the fruit. Macerate for at least an hour or overnight. Sprinkle pistachio nuts over just before serving.

## Pineapple Jelly

Jellies are an excellent way to serve a fruit course since they can be made the day before. There is a wide variety of shapes and sizes of molds to choose from. I prefer to macerate fruit in some sort of spirit to give it an extra flavor.

3     cups canned pineapple purée
2     tablespoons white rum
1     cup orange juice
2     envelopes gelatin
      Mint leaves

Macerate the pineapple in the rum for an hour. Dissolve gelatin in the orange juice by placing it in a small bowl in a pan of simmering water Mix gelatin mixture into the pineapple purée. Pour into a well-oiled mold. Refrigerate for at least 4 hours. Before serving, unmold the jelly and decorate with mint leaves.

## Orange Mousse

This delicious dessert needs to be made at least 4 hours before serving. Make it the day before to give you less to do on the big day.

      Zest of 2 oranges
1/3   cup orange juice
2     eggs, separated
1     egg
1     cup superfine sugar
1     cup heavy cream
      Thickly shredded coconut

Mix the zest and orange juice with 2 beaten egg yolks. Add whole egg and ½ cup of the sugar. Stir over a double boiler for 10 minutes or until it begins to thicken. (If you do not have a double boiler, put a small saucepan inside a large saucepan of simmering water). When cool, refrigerate for 30 minutes.

Beat 2 egg whites until stiff and then beat in half the remaining sugar. Now beat cream with the remainder of sugar until it is stiff. Fold the cream carefully into the egg mixture. Fold in the lime mixture last of all. Pour into an oiled metal mold. Freeze until needed. The mousse should be taken out of the freezer about 15 minutes before it is served. Unmold and sprinkle coconut over the top.

 *COOK'S NOTES: Fruits are transformed by the grilling process into the most delectable desserts. Grill them in their skins, lightly scoring them so they can expand without bursting.*

*I never tire of traditional baked apples. Put them onto the coals straight after the main course is cooked. They are excellent to accompany pork and chicken dishes as well.*

## Baked Apples

A perennial favorite, but this recipe has a few extras you may not have tried before. Serve with ice-cream or yogurt.

| 6 | large cooking apples |
| 1 | cup sultanas |
| 1/2 | cup figs, chopped |
| 1/2 | teaspoon ground ginger |
| 1 | teaspoon ground cinnamon |
| 1/2 | teaspoon ground cloves |
| | Brandy to measure |
| 1/4 | cup butter |
| 1/4 | cup dark brown sugar |

Put sultanas, figs and spices into a jar and cover with the brandy. Leave overnight to macerate. Wash the apples, core them and score a line around the middle to prevent skins bursting. Put them into a shallow ovenproof dish. Stuff sultanas and figs into the apples. Sprinkle with sugar and pour any leftover brandy into the dish. Place a knob of butter on top of each apple and cook in a covered barbecue for about 45 minutes.

# INDEX

Page numbers in **bold** type indicate illustrations.

Aïoli 9
apples, baked 47, **47**
aromatic: general 7
artichokes, barbecued 42
Barbecue sauce 20
bean & tomato salad 44
beef: beef steaks 21
  hamburgers 26
  roast sirloin 18, **19**
  beef teriyaki 21
bruschetta 14
Carrot: & potato dip 12, **12**
  barbecued carrots 40
chicken:
  coconut chicken 30
  glazed chicken wings 33
  Italian grilled **32**, 33
  Japanese chicken kebabs **6**, 34
  mango chicken 31
  tandoori chicken 30, **31**
chili & tomato sauce 9
chocolate bananas 45
corn on the cob, barbecued 40
crudités 9, 10, **11**
Damper 14, **15**
duck, spicy 34
Eggplant:
  baked **16**, 42
  salad 10
Fish: barbecued trout **38**
  barbecued tuna steaks 38
  seafood kebabs 36
  snapper with cilantro 36, **37**
  trout in newspaper 36
five-spice powder 22
fruit: on skewers 45
  sauce 23
  summer berries 45
Garam masala 31
garlic: barbecued 42

sauce 10
grapefruit: orange & grapefruit
  salad 46
Hamburgers 26
Kebabs: general 23, 26
  fruit on skewers 45
  Greek (souvlakia) 26, **27**
  Indian lamb 23
  Italian mixed grill 23
  Japanese chicken 34
  mozzarella & bread skewers 13
  quail & liver skewers 26
  seafood 36
kofta 29
Lamb: butterflied leg of 17
  chops, tandoori-style 18
  Indian lamb kebabs 23
  kofta 29
  Moroccan brochettes 29
  Moroccan leg of **16**, 17
  with thyme & garlic 16
lobster, grilled 39
Marinades: general 8
mixed grill: general 23
  Italian 23
  quail & liver skewers 26
Moroccan brochettes 29
mozzarella & bread skewers 13
mulled wine 14
mushrooms, barbecued 40
Olivade 10
onions, barbecued 40
orange: & grapefruit salad 46
  granita 15, **24-25**
  mousse 46
oysters in the shell 11
Parsnips, barbecued 40
pineapple jelly 46
pork: barbecued spareribs 22
  country-style pork chops **2**, 22

quail & pork liver skewers 26
  spicy sausages **28**, 29
  Vietnamese spareribs 22
potato: barbecued 40
  carrot & potato dip 12, **12**
  poussin, grilled 34
pumpkin, baked with ginger 42
Quail & liver skewers 26
Satays (see kebabs)
sauces: aïoli 9
  barbecue 20
  chili & tomato 9
  fruit 23
  garlic 10
  tarator 10, **11**
  vinaigrette 9
sausages, spicy **28**, 29
shellfish: barbecued garlic shrimp 39
  grilled lobster 39
  oysters in the shell 11
  seafood kebabs 36
shrimp: barbecued garlic 39
souvlakia 26, **27**
summer berries 45
sweet peppers: barbecued 40
sweet potatoes, barbecued 40
Tabbouleh 44, **44**
tarator sauce 10
tomatoes: baked 42, **43**
  bean & tomato salad 44
  chili & tomato sauce 9
turnips, barbecued 40
Veal: rosemary veal chops **20**, 21
  spicy sausages **28**, 29
vegetables: general 40, 42
  barbecued 40, **41**
vinaigrette 9
Yogurt: cold yogurt soup 13
  spicy yogurt salad 43